Women of Power II

Compiled By

Dr. Victoria Sheffield

Mama for
Thanks for
your love X
Support
xoxoxo

ISBN (9781095294345) Printed in USA – Additional copies can be
purchased by emailing us at sheffieldvictoria39@gmail.com

Dedication

I would like to dedicate this book back to God. He is the one that gave the inspiration and the strength to finally share my story. I thank God for giving me the strength to look past what family may think. Knowing that my story will not only bring healing to myself but to others is my inspiration. I dedicate this back to God so that he will get the glory.

I dedicate it to all the hurting families and women that are scarred by the wounds of being abused. I dedicate this back to any person that is dealing with any kind of trauma from their past. I do understand that men can be victims too. I pray that each person that reads this will find hope and peace in their situation. If you are someone today dealing with anger issues, I pray that you will get the help you need. As you are hurting you continue to hurt the people that love you.

(Special Thanks to the Contributing Authors)

Introduction

As women we always seem to press through. We are much more powerful than we know. It is until we go through adversity that we realize that we have the power to tread upon serpents. (Luke 10:19) We've accomplished things we thought we would never do. We made it through childbirth and much more. So many things have challenged us, but we manage to stay strong. We are natural nurturers and anointed to manage the home. We know how to budget a dime on a shoestring income. Before hamburger helper existed a one dish meal was nothing new. Yes, we are much more alike than we are different. We share some of the same sorrows and joys. From changing diapers to combing hair we do what it takes to make things happen.

As the weaker vessel life for a woman will never be easy. A powerful woman of God finds out how to tap into her inner strength. Women of Power II is a testimonial of trials, triumphs, and victories from myself and the other contributing authors. You'll find the hope and encouragement you need to endure.

Hallelujah I'm No Longer Bound

There's No More Chains Holding Me!

As early as I can remember my home was troubled because of the abuse that my mother endured. My father would be the one that physically and emotionally abused her for more than twenty years. Growing up this was all I knew. If you're wondering if there were any good days at all this just depended upon his mood. I knew from a child how to live a life of fear. I knew what it was to suffer at an early age. The sound of his voice and his harsh ways not only wounded me but made me the person I was. Men and women are abused every day, but I speak in the little girl's voice that speaks from the heart of children brought up in such chaos. One of my vivid memories was when my parent's pastor found out about the abuse. Dad would beat my mom during the week then take us to church on Sunday. Not to mention the fact that he would occasionally deliver the Sunday message. The pastor finding out would be another thing that would set him off. I remember the pastor did what any good pastor should have. He sat my father down by not allowing him to speak again. My father's anger caused him to throw away all my mom's gospel albums. It would be years before we went to church again. My mother did not have a car and driving one of his was forbidden. My mother was never the type to argue or fight back. All she ever knew was how to survive. She married young at the age of eighteen and at my birth. Just in case you are someone wondering if I have siblings, I have an older sister and two younger brothers.

In both grade school and high school, I was quiet and afraid to talk to most people. As a child many of us that suffered trauma was taught "**What Goes on in the House, Stays in the House**". We were trained to hold in our emotions. Very few people in our circle knew what was going on in our home. My father had to be one of the meanest people that I knew. We had those moments that felt normal until his personality would shift. Did I mention the fact that he was a Vietnam War Veteran? Some of them came back from war changed—shell shocked. Interesting enough the enemy had him bound and he had us bound too. When I look at it now, our situation seemed controlled and felt somewhat as if we were in boot camp. I remember a time when he got mad and fussed at me because he told me to wash the light-colored clothes. I did not know in his mind this meant all white clothes. He fussed if the grass grew too tall or short. When he came home each day, I would run to my room and close the door real fast. I knew that once he entered our home, things would change. Our home never felt like a happy home in my opinion. There were even days that I wished he was dead. Sadly, I learned how to hate as a teen but deep in my heart I knew I loved my daddy. What I want everyone to know is that I grew up scared of my own father. Our entire infrastructure was wack. The family unit was tainted. When the head of any home is out-of-place, everyone hurts. The enemy used my father's background to try to destroy us. Do I feel as if he loved us? I don't feel as if he knew how to. He was drafted in the military at age eighteen and saw things that no one should. Truth-be-told, sometimes people are sent home from the military traumatized themselves with no rehabilitation. I was affected in many ways but the one thing that stood out the most was the fact that I was afraid of living life and being sociable. I was so shy in kindergarten that the school recommended that I be put in special needs class. Some would say I am or was shy too, but I was abnormally quiet. The enemy had my mouth shut. I was so bashful that instead of doing oral reports in school I would refuse and take an F. There were a few people that I did talk to like my mom, close friends, and close family. One of my close friends from grade school is still near and dear to my heart today. We must have been in the seventh grade. I will never forget the time that she got so frustrated with me at school and said, "girl you're gonna talk to me". At that moment something broke in me. I felt so comfortable with her that we became even closer. I see today that there are those people that God places in our life for specific reasons. I realize now that I talked only to those that I felt very comfortable with. No one had ever confronted me like that before. I even started talking to other friends more though I was still broken. By the time I went off to high school I had more friends but was still very quiet. I always seemed to feel inadequate around the popular kids. I was in a shell but in many ways your average teenager. My friends and I partied but I found it hard to date because I would never communicate with my boyfriends. I mean we talked but I was always the type to bottle up emotions. When I think about it, I understand that everyone has patterns. Patterns are simply just the way people handle emotions and repeat behaviors. My way of handling life's ups and downs was to keep it all in. What I learned to do in childhood, I took into adulthood. Often, I wanted to be the bold person that I saw in other people. I was merely existing and not living.

As a teen I found a passion. I absolutely loved to dance. I was a cheerleader in the eighth grade. I was on the drill team for three years and even made captain my senior year. Dance helped me channel my emotions but there was still a void in my life. My last year of high school a good friend asked me to go to church with her. I enjoyed visiting her church so much that I started going more. I still partied with friends but enjoyed the worship experience. I had no idea that this would be the beginning of me establishing a relationship with God. I would be the only one in my family going to church. I graduated from high school then went to trade school. At this point in my life I noticed that partying had started getting boring. I was now about the age of twenty and still in my parent's home. I was miserable and just did not like my father. In fact, we would pass each other and never speak. The home felt broken and I felt alone. Mom later bought her first car with money she saved from sewing for her clients. She even started back going to church periodically. I began to love God so much that I would eventually join the church and get saved. For the first time in my life something felt right. I eventually got married and knew that I wanted something different for my own kids. I tried very hard to make a happy home for them.

My mom's life took a turn when she started partying. This would be totally out of character for her. I think that after her children started moving out of the home, she just lost sight of who she was. She was still in the home with him even though he stopped hitting her. He still had a lot of his ways and I am sure that living with him still wasn't easy. I remember God dealing with me about praying for my family. I even remember dreaming about a burning bush. When I asked God why I'd had this dream, he told me that he would use me to bring my family out of bondage. I knew that those that wanted to be set free through my prayers would be. Though I was saved, I still had wounds from my past. I found it hard to trust people and to talk to people that hurt me. I would later be called into ministry but ran from the calling for many years. I felt so inadequate from my past that I just did not feel as if I could handle the call. I was the same girl that would take the F in school so preaching was the last thing that I felt I could do. I was so horrified of speaking in front of people that my heart fluctuated. Many years I hid myself working in children's ministries to avoid my calling. I love children dearly, but I hoped that if I hid myself in children's church that hopefully no one would see my calling. What I want people to know is that when we walk in disobedience, there is a void. I believe that when we are not doing what we are called to do, we feel out of place. Many years I lived in the belly of the big fish (disobedience). I can't honestly tell people how many years went by before I answered the call. I am sure that ten to fifteen years went by or even more. After going through many years of this God pretty much whipped my behind. Thank God I finally stop running. I went through a series of trials and tribulations that God would allow me to go through. I am sure that God knows how to gain our attention. I'd always done outreach ministry, but it was when I wrote my purple book "It's Been a Long Journey" that I decided to walk in boldness. God told me to write this book so that people could see who I was as a spirit filled woman. I had hidden myself from so many people that most people did not know who I was. That book even shares intimate details about spiritual encounters I've had with God.

I had to start believing that I was the person that God called me to be. If we don't view ourselves as great others won't. We all have a great assignment because we were created in the image of God. Each time I accepted a speaking engagement or decided to do a live video on social media, I became stronger and stronger. Today I am thriving because I am walking in obedience doing what God has called me to do. Before I was born the enemy had it out for me and still does. I am not worried because I am covered by the blood and the blood still works! Today that same little shy timid girl has her own radio broadcast and network. I am no longer bound or locked up in chains. Never again will I allow the enemy to hold me captive. If you are someone dealing with wounds of the past, walk in boldness by pulling down strongholds in your life. **2 Corinthians 10:3-5** ³For though we walk in the flesh, we do not war after the flesh: (For the weapons of our warfare are not carnal, but mighty through God to the **pulling** down of strongholds;) Casting **down** imaginations, and every high thing that exalteth itself against the knowledge of God, and bringing into captivity every thought to the obedience of Christ;

It's not God's will for us to live the defeated life. The enemy has a hit on our life because he doesn't want us to be used by God. He uses our past and anything else he can to deter us from our destiny. That's why we must walk in obedience by pressing through the pain. We must learn how to pull those strongholds down to subjection. We can do this by praying, praising, and using the power that God has given us though his word. When our trials seem unbearable, we should pray. We should praise when the devil feels as if he is winning. We must have faith understanding that there is power in the name of Jesus. We should learn how to cast our cares upon him and believe that he will see us through. When we cast our cares upon him it is vital not to take those things back. Leave them on the alter and understand that Jesus paid the ultimate price.

I had to learn how to speak the word of God over my own life. When the enemy told me what I couldn't do, I told him that I could do all things through Christ that strengthens me. In other words, throw the word back at him.

Do this as soon as you feel or hear negativity. That's why it is important to **STAY IN THE WORD**. Read it **EVEN WHEN YOU DON'T FEEL LIKE IT. The word of God brings healing and deliverance!** Eat it, meditate on it, speak it, and receive it! Keep doing this **until** you are set free. Then when you are, stay in there (the word) because the enemy comes in like a flood seeking whom he may devour. Remember his job is to kill, steal, and destroy. He won't be happy for you when you are soaring!! Satan is a defeated foe—powerless in terms of the word of God. God is using Chain Breaking Ministries and my other ministries to set captives free. I am now walking in boldness not afraid to be me. There are times while praying that I've seen in the spirit chains falling off the people I pray for. God gave me this ministry to help others be set free too. I am rejoicing and praising God because I now know my worth. The enemy made me feel worthless. Even when I was overlooked in ministries, God was raising me up. He took my dry dead bones and gave me life. When they talk about you and turn their backs on you know that God has you wrapped up in his arms. God won't send you out as sheep amongst wolves then leave you. He'll hold you up when you feel as if you are falling. When you are being abused, lied on, talked about, and misunderstood, he is a friend that will stick closer than any other. He has given us his word which is all the spiritual ammunition that we need. Ephesians Chapter 6 verse 17 says "And take the helmet of salvation, and the sword of the Spirit, which is the word of God:"

God gave me my own ministry and told me not to worry about those that pretended to not see my calling. He knew that if he gave me my own that I could not use this as an excuse anymore. Are you afraid to be who God called you to be? Read Jeremiah Chapter 1 in the bible. Before you entered your mother's womb, God knew you and called you forth for such a time as this. It is time for you to move!!! Prepare yourself for the journey because preparation is the key to success. As you are reading this, I supernaturally speak life into every dead and dry thing in your body. There is always hope in Christ. Stop feeling as if tomorrow I will walk in the authority that God has given to me. Tomorrow is not promised to us. You **Be Bold** and **Be You** today knowing that God has called you to greatness. He created you unique and wants you to use every gift that he has given you. If no one else believes in you, believe in yourself and know that God is with you. I call forth your spiritual baby and challenge you to move in the things of God. When you move, God will bless you, elevate you, and provide everything you need to fulfill his glory!! Woman or man of God don't worry about falling because if you do, God is there to catch you!!! **Deuteronomy 31:8** The LORD himself goes before you and will be with you; he **will never leave you nor forsake you**. Do not be afraid; do not be discouraged."

Matthew 19:30 But many who are first will be last, and many who are last will be first.

Journal Your Thoughts About My Testimony

_____

_____

_____

_____

_____

_____

_____

_____

_____

_____

_____

_____

_____

_____

_____

_____

_____

_____

Pastor Jacqueline Goodwin

"I Shall Live and Not Die"

I shall not die, but live, and declare the works of the LORD. Psalm 118:17

I was destined for greatness but had to travel through pain, humiliation, and death to arrive at my ordained place. From the time of my conception, the enemy saw a vessel being born that would change the nation. He devised a plan to kill me but God spoke and said, "Before I formed thee in the belly I knew thee; and before thou camest forth out of the womb I sanctified thee, and I ordained thee a prophet unto the nations" (Jeremiah 1: 5). My mother told me before she found out she was pregnant with me she thought she was constipated and asked my grandfather for some good old-fashioned turpentine. After completing a bottle, she felt no different. She then decided to go see her doctor only to discover that she was carrying me. She immediately told her doctor that she was taking turpentine and inquired about the side effects. Her doctor was amazed that the seed she was carrying had survived. The devil had planned to kill me but my mother, who was an intercessor covered me under the blood. When God's hand is on your life there is nothing satan can do to stop it. Don't think his attempt stopped there. This was only the beginning of my battle. At the age of three, my mother taught me about fasting and praying. She provided me with the tools that would sustain my very life to the age of thirty-five. God always prepares you for your test. I became sick with a cold that I could not get rid of. I decided to buy some over-the-counter medicine. I took the medication only to learn that I was not getting better. I decided to go to the doctor. When I arrived at the doctor's office, I was in a good mood. On the way there I spent some time with God not knowing what was lying ahead for me. Afterward, I got called back to see the doctor. After his examination, he informed me that my diagnosis was HIV.

Hallelujah! As I sat there on the table and looked at the door all I could see was Jesus hanging on the cross for me. I politely picked up my pocketbook and said to my doctor, "It is well." On the way out I stopped to ask my prayer partner who worked there to touch and agree with me. There is nothing like a praying woman of God in your corner. She immediately got up from behind her desk and prayed. She told me that all she could hear was God saying, " Isaiah 43:2: "When thou passest through the waters, I will be with thee; and through the rivers, they shall not overflow thee; when thou walkest through the fire, thou shalt not be burned; neither shall the flame kindle upon thee." When she finished praying, I began to thank God in advance for my healing. As I drove home, God instructed me to go on a three-day fast. God told me not to talk on the cell or house phone and to have no visitors. As for my mother who was a phenomenal prayer warrior, God said just ask her to cover you while you are on this fast. God is faithful! As I went on a shutdown, I boldly went to the throne. I told God that surely if you were able to raise Lazarus from the grave after being dead for four days, HIV is nothing for you to heal. I told God I'm coming like Hezekiah with my face to the wall and I am on death row awaiting my execution. I told God that he was the only one who could take me off death row. I said, "Lord, I want to see my children's, children's, children grow up." God spoke and said, "You shall live and not die." God then revealed to me where the man who had infected me was hiding his medicine. I told this man that he had allowed the devil to use him to try to take me out, but God would never leave his daughter in the dark. He would get the GLORY!

During my fast, I sought God day and night expecting my miracle. I told God if I had to lie on my face 160 days I would because I was not moving until my healing came. Glory Jesus! On the third day of my fast God woke me up and showed me the words: **NEGATIVE AND VICTORY!** I called my doctor and told him I needed more blood work done and he told me I was in denial. I told him that I was not in denial but healed and set free. Hallelujah! When the results came back it was NEGATIVE! God is Faithful! God told me to go on a thirty-day fast for this man and I was obedient. It was then I knew that I had the love of Jesus down in my heart and soul. I stayed before God seeking his healing. On the twenty-eighth day the young man started acting up! How many of you know that before the breakthrough the devil must kick up!? My spirit was willing, but my body was tired of his attitude. I got into my flesh and started to throw in the towel. As I was getting ready to do that, God intervened before he allowed his word not to come to pass. He sent a woman of

God to remind me of the instructions He gave me to follow.

I heard the doorbell ring and at the door was one of my prayer partners. She said to me, "Prophetess, I don't know what this means, but God told me to come to your house and tell you to continue to fast and pray for him." I fell on my face and cried out to my Father. I said, "Daddy, I need your strength because I can't complete this task without you. Oh Daddy, I need you to make this man do four things: lie down like the lion in Daniel's den, eat, and take a bath and go to sleep." Guess what? He did those four things. My mother and my prayer partner began praying for me and I felt the anointing coming all over me. I told God I was ready to do what he had required of me. I anointed every piece of clothes and shoes he had. I pleaded the blood of Jesus in and outside my house. I pleaded the blood of Jesus in every room in my house and over me and my children. On the thirtieth day, God woke me at 3:00 a.m. and told me to lay my hands on his forehead and call HIV out in the name of Jesus. The more I called it out, the hotter his temperature got. I began to speak in my heavenly language. God revealed to me the reason why he was hot was because HIV was coming out of his body. Glory Jesus! God healed our bodies! God is JEHOVAH ROPHE! God gave me a revelation for the diagnosis called AIDS. God said that it stands for "Appearing Impossible but Dying to Surrender!" He also gave me a revelation for HIV. He said, it stands for "Healing in the Vessel." I became a vessel who had to die from my flesh and surrender totally to God for my healing.

I encourage you, if you have been diagnosed with cancer, diabetes, or high blood pressure, don't stop fasting and believing in God. Cry out unto the Lord because he will heal your body. My mother, who was diagnosed with kidney failure, diabetes, and high blood pressure, never gave up on God! She spoke everyday whether at home or at dialysis that she was healed. Her favorite words to me were, "Jackie I'm going to trust in the Lord until I die!" At the beginning of 2008 God gave me a prophetic word for my mom. He told me to tell her that year would be the year of her total healing. God began making her eyesight clearer so she could read her bible again. Next, her blood pressure became regulated. Her last request was for her kidneys to be healed. God kept his promise. On

October 17, 2008, my mother was healed totally. She went home to be with the Lord. That night I asked God to show me how she looked in her new body. A slew of white doves covered my room and I felt the anointing of the doves, the holiness, and peace. The only thing I could do was get on my knees and give reverence to God.

Psalm 62:6 Truly he is my rock and my salvation; he is my fortress, I will not be shaken.

Journal Your Thoughts About Her Testimony

_____

_____

_____

_____

_____

_____

_____

_____

_____

_____

_____

_____

_____

_____

_____

_____

_____

_____

_____

Martavia (Sharee) Houston

I was born July 31 in Germany. At the age of five I moved to Miami, Florida. Growing up, I faced many challenges. Some were out of my control and others perfectly within my control. Never-the-less I was determined life would not get the best of me. God had something greater for my life even if I couldn't see it. At this point of my life, it was time to start believing in myself. For whatever reason, I never seemed to really fit in. Life had stripped me down of my innocents early on. Even in my rebellious stages, I knew God wanted to do more with my life. I knew that my experiences would one day help others. I was a teenage mom when I gave birth to my son Marcus in June 2001. I did not let this stop me. Despite the difficulties I faced with being a young mother, I still overcame and was determined not to be a statistic. I finished high school and graduated a year early. My great grandmother and best friend was my biggest cheerleader. She would often call me college girl every step of the way.

Soon after, I moved out of my mom's house into my own apartment. This was an opportunity to learn more of life lessons. I experienced domestic violence a few times and betrayal. I was used, abused, and treated like I was nothing. My heart was broken leading me to lose sight of myself and my worth. Even in this, I always accomplished what I set my mind to. That gift of perseverance is my driving force in all that I accomplish. After my high school love went on to the army, I met someone else and fell in love again. January 2005, I birthed my second child Dyani. Eventually I saw the need to do something different with my life and decided to move to Georgia in late fall of 2006. I wanted to purchase a home and offer a better life for my children. A few years later February 14, 2008, I married the father of my oldest daughter. March 2008, I purchased my first home and strived at being the best wife and mother I could be while still trying to find my purpose. Through the trials and tribulations in my life, I continued to stand strong and push forward. Blow after blow, I kept getting back up and fighting knowing that there was great potential on my life. There were many times I cried and wanted to quit but because of my children, I continued to stand.

Eventually, my marriage ended and once again I had to find my way. I had a health scare in 2009 and ended up in ICU for a week.

My vitals were 77/36. After being released from the hospital I decided that there had to be more to my life than failure and pain. I made a declaration to be better by doing better. I began to surround myself with positive people and built a spiritual circle to keep me grounded and accountable. At this time, I knew that I could take off like an eagle and soar. I decided to go to school. I obtained a bachelor's degree in Business Management. I became active in my church at Berean Christian Church Gwinnett where Pastor Kevin B. Lee is my pastor and spiritual father. I successfully completed the class titled Master Life under Deacon Willie and Renee Robinson. I gained a new understanding of how to allow God to be the master of my life. I started working hands-on with children realizing the true gems they are in God. Continuing to soar, I established my own business called Motivated Under the Sun. Through this business, I'm able to reach out to my community constantly. The goal is to find ways to give back as well as mentor the youth. In 2011, the enemy would attempt to take my life again. My car flipped off the road as I was taking my children to visit family in Miami. This near-death experience opened my eyes even more. I promised myself to be more intentional and not take a second of life for granted. Then April 2013, I was attacked again when I had to have an emergency blood transfusion. I was having heart palpitations due to not having enough blood for my heart to pump. I sat in the hospital wondering and asked myself why God would save my life once again.

Fast-forward to January 2015, when I had my third child and miracle, Princess Paris. My goodness was this pregnancy a rocky one. The doctors told me the child was dead then came back later and confirmed that I was eight weeks pregnant. At her birth, doctors informed me that she would need emergency surgery because her intestines were enlarged. Never-the-less, what a mighty God we serve! She did have surgery at three months but no other issues afterward. I still wouldn't trade any of it for the world because it strengthened my relationship with God. This took my faith to another level. I have a passion for empowering women and especially those that are hurting. I work with Young Woman of Worth alongside Donna Price. I'm able to use my experiences and testimony to assist other women. Another area where I give back is working with the youth of the Believe in Me Project with my spiritual mother, Juanita Thompson. God is using me to give teenage moms hope. I even assist in the area of helping victims of domestic violence and victims of sexual abuse find their voice. In January 2016, I accepted my new assignment to help at-risk youth in ISS (Indoor School Suspension). It was there where I met an amazing earthly angel by the name of Thelma Armstrong. She helped guide me through with her wisdom and unconditional love. Through this assignment, I've been able to touch the lives of many students and their families. My passion has always been towards people and finding out how I can be of service to others. I am now riding the wave of life in this new chapter and season. I am preparing my first blessing for college in the fall. The second blessing I am preparing for freshmen year in high school. My little princess and miracle is being prepared for pre-kindergarten. Even though I still have my struggles, I manage to continue being a blessing to others. Life has been rough for me, but I will keep on trusting God to carry me through. Despite the health scares and all that i've been through, I know that it ain't over until God says it is! I am grateful to finally know the true meaning of self-love. I am serious about the purpose God has placed into the core of my soul. Especially after my last couple of health scares. I took an oath with God to go full force into my calling while letting God order every one of my steps. I am determined to let God use my life experiences for his glory!

Proverbs 31:10 Who can find a virtuous woman? for her price is far above rubies.

Journal Your Thoughts About Her Testimony

_____

_____

_____

_____

_____

_____

_____

_____

_____

_____

_____

_____

_____

_____

_____

_____

_____

_____

_____

_____

_____

Bobbie Tomlin

I've never said this out loud to anyone. This is the first time that I've had the courage to express this without the feeling of being judged. Knowing how the world can be, I pray that I am able to prevent others from making the same choices I made. Some that led up to these events. During the summer of "95" we had just gotten some new neighbors that seemed pretty nice. They were a married couple about in their late thirties. The week they moved in I finally got the opportunity to meet them. My mom introduced them to me and told me that she and the neighbor's husband had the same birthday. I thought to myself "if he's anything like you I'd rather not even get to know him!" I hated my mom!! She abused me from as far back as I could remember. Whenever I did anything right (her way) she would find any reason to mistreat me. She would hit me or take something away from me. She would say things like "oh you didn't wash the dishes or I'm going to whoop your behind". Most of the time I wouldn't be doing anything wrong other than my homework. Embrace yourself because there is more of my story!

So as time went on the neighbors and my family had gotten close. By the time the next year came they were pretty much a part of the family. It was my twelfth birthday on July 21st, 1996. It was nothing usual about me not getting a gift or doing anything special. That morning, my mom told me that I was going to work with the neighbor Daniel. She told me that I would help him clean up some stuff and he would pay me. I said, "Do I really have to go"? It's my birthday and I would rather just sit at home. She said, "No you always want stuff". "You better go make that money because I don't have any money to buy you nothing." Either way I had to go whether I wanted to go or not. Daniel and I left at about ten am and we went to one of the houses he had just finished remodeling. He had his own construction company. I got the stuff out the truck so that I could go in and start cleaning. Then I stood in the door waiting for him to open it. I immediately started cleaning the kitchen while he was doing whatever he had to do. I'm not real sure how much time went by because I had on my headphones. I think maybe about three hours went by. I finally ended up cleaning the back room. I was on the floor on my knees scrubbing this stain up out the carpet and before I knew it, he had rushed me and flipped me over. I was on my back lying on the floor and he was on top of me trying to take my clothes off. I didn't scream because he had this look in his eyes that scared me so badly. I took a deep breath and I said "please get off of me and stop before I" quickly interrupting me he says "if you scream I'll choke you and you know you can't tell your momma because she isn't going to believe anything you say!" I just laid there and cried as he raped me. After it was over, he seemed to be so disgusted with me. He wouldn't look at me or even talk to me. He even made me ride in the back seat. When I got home, I didn't say anything because he was absolutely right, my mom would always take his word over mine. The sad thing is that she'd take anyone's word over mine. I went in the house as she went outside. They talked for a while because she didn't come in the house for about two hours. I sat in the shower and cried. I felt so horrible and filthy that I scrubbed myself over and over again. I scrubbed so hard until my skin started to peel. After I started peeling, I got out, dried off, and went to sleep. I didn't have anyone to talk to because I had no friends or no family that I was close with. After about two weeks of being sad, I kind of just sucked it up. Unfortunately, I was accustomed to being mistreated. I was good at suppressing stuff and acted as if nothing had happened.

Now I will fast-forward about six years later, at the age of eighteen. I was living a promiscuous life with men and women. One day in late August 2002 I had just started college and met this guy that was great, so I thought. We had become inseparable. After about nine months together he sat me down one day and said, "I've noticed that you don't like to talk to me about stuff and I see that when we have sex, you're always closing your eyes". "It seems as if you're not really there". "Can you tell me what I need to do in order to make things better between us?" I just apologized and told him that I would do better. I knew exactly what the problem was but of course I wasn't about to talk to him about all the men and women I had been sleeping with. Quite naturally I didn't want to talk about the ones that I had been with while we were together. I just started to change my behavior so that he wouldn't mention it again. Just as I thought, it didn't work. About a month later he asked me "why do you close your eyes during sex?" I said, "don't know, I just do it". He responded and said, "the next time we have sex can you try and look at me"? I said "ok." Later that night while we were having sex of course I tried to open my eyes, but it was impossible! I broke down in tears and ran into the bathroom and locked the door. He knocked on the door saying "Bobbie, please let me in". "Please tell me what I did wrong"? "Please don't cry just talk to me." I stayed in the bathroom until morning because I could not look at him. That dirty feeling had come back to haunt me. I felt the emotions all over again. I felt the same sadness. I started self-blaming and wished I was dead. After he left for work, I went to the liquor store and bought a bottle of vodka. After that I got a refill on my ibprophen and went home. I cried all the way home. I can't even remember if I parked correctly in the parking space when I got to the apartment building. I rushed into the door and ran into the bathroom. I opened the liquor bottle and began downing the pills and the vodka together. The bottle was finally empty and so was the liquor bottle. I laid on the floor and closed my eyes. I'm not sure the time frame, but I woke up to my boyfriend's finger being shoved down my throat. I was throwing up so badly all over the floor. I could hear him saying

"Good baby, just keep pushing it out"! "Open your eyes baby girl look at me". He said, "I'm about to call the ambulance just hold on baby"! By the time the paramedics arrived I was alert and looking well. I refused to go to the hospital and stayed home. They left and he sat on the floor and said, "baby talk to me why would you do this"? "Can we please just drive to the ER"? I said "NO!! I'm fine." I started crying again. He just held me and laid on the floor with me all night. The next morning, I told him everything and he just said he was so sorry that it happened. The blessing is that he left work early and decided to come home early. He mentioned that he was so glad that he decided to leave work early yesterday.

Even though we aren't together now, I thank God for him being in my life. I wanted to die because I thought I was worthless and had no purpose. I thought that the rape was my fault. I would always say things like if I didn't or I should not have. **My biggest mistake was not ever saying anything to anyone.** I guess it worked out in my favor because when I finally decided to tell my mom she said, "well that's not what Daniel told me". That alone would have made me want to die again! I have forgiven him and can even look at him without feeling anything. As for my mother, I'm still working on that forgiveness. I do feel that God kept me alive for a reason. I feel like there are so many young girls that are going through what I went through. I want them to learn to love themselves because sometimes it will feel like no one loves them. Going through this makes victims feel alone. I want to help young ladies that have abusive parents learn that the abuse was not their fault. I want to empower them so that they can rise to their fullest potential. This way they can see that God did have a plan for their life and the enemy did not win! I just want God to use me in any way that he feels necessary to save the lives of young girls.

Psalm 23:4 Yea, though I walk through the valley of the shadow of death, I will fear no evil: for thou art with me; thy rod and thy staff they comfort me.

Journal Your Thoughts About Her Testimony

_____

_____

_____

_____

_____

_____

_____

_____

_____

_____

_____

_____

_____

_____

_____

_____

_____

_____

_____

_____

_____

_____

Kutuna Council

I have always had a confident attitude and optimistic look on life. Looking at me, you can't tell what I've been through. I have a business that I established back in 2011 called Divalyfe. The business often put me in front of the camera, modeling my own product. In the nineties, people told me that I favored the singer Brandy but honestly, I don't see it. I believe that this is due to the fact that we have similar facial structures, and both wore micro braids back then. I'm an average height lady with medium brown skin. What makes me stand out is my youthful appearance and the fact that I always wear my own brand. Even though we're twenty years apart, strangers always think my daughter and I are sisters. I always tried to keep a smile on my face so that people never knew what I felt on the inside. I've learned to push through my trials. That's something I learned to do from my grandmother Thelma.

At birth I faced trials and tribulations. Doctors diagnosed me with Hemoglobin SC Disease. This means that both of my parents had either the Sickle Cell trait or disease. Back then it was simply known as Sickle Cell Disease. Sickle Cell is a blood condition that causes my red blood cells to be shaped like a sickle instead of round. The sickle-shaped red blood cells have trouble moving through my blood vessels which not only causes pain but also low oxygen levels that makes me fatigued, dizzy, and sometimes hinders my ability to concentrate. I'm in pain every day and it's so intense that the daily pain turns into crisis. Crisis pain paralyzes the body. It feels like someone is stabbing my bones and constricting my muscles.

I was born and raised in Palatka, Florida a small town on the coast of the St. Johns River. This was one of my favorite places to go growing up. I still enjoy going there because of the town's dock. People are always down there fishing. It's considered downtown but it's truly the heart of the city. There are boat races, and the annual Azalea & Blue Crab festivals that come to town around the Spring. I always remember being surrounded by family. We lived in a project on Napoleon & 16th street before moving as our family grew bigger. My grandmother was the head of the household. She raised six kids. Almost all of them lived at home along with my brother and myself. My condition caused major concern with my grandmother. Her concern was due to my mom being her wild sagittarius child. My mother was hardly ever home. My mother ended up getting pregnant with me while in vocational school studying to become a chef. My grandma pretty much knew that she was going to be the one to take care of me. This caused many arguments usually ending with my mom leaving for days and even weeks at a time. When she returned home, they argued even more because of her absence.

My grandmother, Thelma Lamb or Tet as everyone called her, was from Alabama. She was born in 1937. She was one of three children. Known as the matriarch of the family, she was undeniably gorgeous with brown mahogany skin and a slim thick figure. She always kept her thin mid-length hair done up in a style and dressed jazzy. She was very protective of me especially when it concerned my mom and other kids in the neighborhood. The fact that I was sick all the time made her even more protective. Tet was the pillar of our community. She was a person everyone loved and respected. Not many people bothered or disrespected her and if you did, you didn't get away with it! Throughout my life, she seldom talked about her childhood. There was this one story I did remember. I remember her telling me about how her father went out to the store one day and never returned. He wasn't a man to walk out on his family. His disappearance was rumored to be the result of a hate crime. A while after that her sister passed away as a teenager. This left her with just one brother, Charlie Willie who is still living to this day as a bus driver and retired postman.

Tet was one of the strong black women in my neighborhood. Back in the day we truly lived by the saying, "It takes a village." Most neighbors were involved in raising each other's kids. I loved this and hated it at the same time. Everyone felt like family, but I could never get away with anything without my grandma finding out. She was the glue that held our family together. She had many friends and was very loved. She was always organizing family cookouts. She loved gatherings! Family and friends would come over and set up tents. We would drink and have music flowing throughout the neighborhood. The kids had just as much fun running around carefree. Our family bond was impressive, yet we had our issues just like any other family. We knew when to let it go and have a good time. Having Sickle Cell, I was often in and out of the hospital. I remember being admitted for crisis pain and blood transfusions. Doctors had me hooked up to what felt like a million tubes and wires. I can't remember what my grandma would say but she was always there holding my hand. She gave me certain looks that made me feel safe and assured that everything would be okay. This was a big part of my life, in and out of the ER and hospital rooms. Tired of being poked and prodded more than anything I wanted to have a normal life. I wanted to do the things I heard my friends talk about like cheerleading and dance classes. Even as I started to be home more than hospital bound, I couldn't do the extracurricular activities I wanted to do, so I did what I could.

When I wasn't in crisis my grandma treated me like any other child from discipline to chores. I believe this is part of the reason I'm so strong and resilient today! She taught me how to pick myself up and keep going after the pain and to even work through it when I must. I passed this trait down to my daughter who doesn't have Sickle Cell disease, but she does have the trait. It isn't as severe as the disease but from what she describes it sounds like she experiences severe pain. When my daughter was born it completely changed my life. I fell in love with this little being that was in an incubator. Her silky straight and jet-black hair grew all the way down to the nape of her neck. I couldn't believe this was my daughter! All I felt for her was unconditional love that would last a lifetime. After having three miscarriages the Lord finally blessed me with my rainbow baby. She was a tiny, perfect, and beautiful miracle. We named her Jasmine after the flower. She was born on March 29th, 1995. This date will always be special to me. It was on this day that I knew I had to make sure my baby felt love. I wanted her to know without a shadow of a doubt that she was loved. It's not an easy journey by far but I've learned to manage it. I'm not sure where I would be without my grandmother's guidance and empowerment. I'm blessed, I'll never have to find out.

Philippians 3:14 ESV - I press on toward the goal for the prize of the upward call of God in Christ Jesus.

Journal Your Thoughts About Her Testimony

_____

_____

_____

_____

_____

_____

_____

_____

_____

_____

_____

_____

_____

_____

_____

_____

_____

_____

_____

Psalm 34:19
Many are the afflictions of the righteous: but the LORD delivereth him out of them all.

God never told us that the road would be easy. As women we've gone through many things but have managed to persevere. God has graced us with the power and ability to endure. Many of us have been knocked down by life but found the strength to rise again. Amazingly, we have been graced with the ability to multiply the universe. When I think about the powerful women of the Bible, I know that God is a rewarder to those that trust and believe. Deborah, a great prophetess and judge lead an army that defeated the Canaanites. Can you imagine a woman leading a great army of men? She was one of great influence in her time. Queen Esther put her life on the line and helped save her people from being killed. King Xerxes who happened to be her husband issued a decree to destroy the Jews. Both women were brave enough to face their giant and faithful enough to believe that he could. They both were God fearing women that stood on his word. He is the same God that prevailed then and will now.

As women we've proven through our testimonies that God is everything we need. He is our rock and source in a time of need. He is a way maker and a burden barrier. I know from experience that he is also a sustainer. He gives us the strength to go through the storms we feel we can't. Not to mention the power we receive after the fire. Some of us have heard it before, "More Pain – More Power" "No Pain – No Power"! The more we go through the greater anointing we will have. We may not understand it all but by and by God's glory is always revealed. I encourage every woman to trust God even when you feel you don't see a trace of him. It's in those moments when he seems quiet when God is up to something great. Focus on him while in tribulation knowing that he just wants to use you. Focus more on what he is saying about your situation than the trial. Know woman of God that God is turning it around for you. So be patient, wait on the Lord, and be of good courage. Walk in victory and boldness claiming your inheritance. God can, will, and is gonna do what his word says. In fact, everything the enemy stole from you including your joy I hear the Lord saying, "I will restore what the canker worms have stolen". Amen!

Stay in his word women of God. Remember that some things come by fasting and prayer. Spend intimate time with him putting him FIRST and watch him move in your life. Some things won't change as we know but God can make it alright and well with you. Remember the serenity prayer and don't forget this: **Ephesians 6**:12-13 King James Version (**KJV**) 12 For we wrestle not against flesh and blood, but against principalities, against powers, against the rulers of the darkness of this world, against spiritual wickedness in high places. That's why when we are faced with calamity, we should rise above what we see in the flesh. This will be the only way we can handle the cares of this world. This means we should get out of the flesh and war in the spirit. We should use the sword of the spirit which is the Word of God. Above all of this, our faith is what will make us whole. Life is an uphill journey, but we can make it if we live right and walk by faith and not by sight. Without faith it is impossible to please God. He knows that if we don't believe we won't stand a chance against the wiles of the enemy. God has given us what we need but we must remember to tap into the power.

Women you are a chosen nation. You are chosen to birth a nation that won't be afraid of the enemy. As women it is important to teach and train our children about the things of God. One day we will leave them. They must know about spiritual warfare. Our children aren't too young to learn about the enemy and his tactics. One thing I have always been passionate about is teaching my children about the things of God. If you are a woman today that has no children, you can still love and nurture a child. It takes God's village to raise up little boys and girls that will fight the good fight of faith. To whom much is given, much is required. Women of God you are chosen to impact this world by sharing your stories as God leads you. Pay-It-Forward by ministering to another woman especially the younger generation. When will we get back to the things that use to work? There was a time when the younger women wouldn't get offended by the older women imparting into their lives. Women of Power, it's time for us to reach back and help those that are loss, bound, and motherless. "Spiritual Moms Birth Spiritual Babies Because Iron Sharpens Iron!!

The Serenity Prayer

God grant me the serenity
to accept the things I cannot change;
courage to change the things I can;
and wisdom to know the difference.
Living one day at a time;
Enjoying one moment at a time;
Accepting hardships as the pathway to peace;
Taking, as He did, this sinful world
as it is, not as I would have it;
Trusting that He will make all things right if I
surrender to His will;
That I may be reasonably happy in this life and
supremely
happy with Him forever in the next.
Amen

A Prayer for Women

Father give us the strength to carry out our daily duties.
Lord I lift up every sister to you in prayer.
When our days seem stressful and full help us to cast our
cares upon you. Show us how to trust and depend
on you in every situation. Father in the name of Jesus we
thank you for keeping us through our trials and
tribulations. We thank you for your glory being revealed.
Even though we do not understand everything we
thank you for your power. We thank you for teaching us
how to warfare. Thank you for helping us to be stronger.
Thank you Lord for giving us the strength to endure. We
thank you for revealing yourself to us. We thank you
for giving us hope and the strength not to give up. Father
in Jesus name help us to support and pray for one
another more. Help us to love each other unconditionally.
We thank you Lord for never leaving us and for
supplying us with our needs. We thank you for what you
have already done. We thank you in advance for what
you will do in our lives. In Jesus Name! Amen!

If You Enjoyed Women of Power II, You'll Enjoy the First Volume

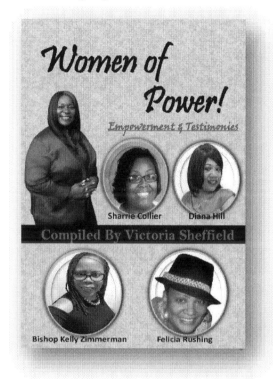

https://amzn.to/2WiPgBW
Do Us a Favor and Leave a Positive Star Review on Amazon! Thanks!

Books Can Also be Purchased Directly From any of the Contributors.

Connect With me on Social to Find Out When Our Next Women of Power Conference Is.

Facebook
https://www.facebook.com/victoria.l.sheffield
Twitter
https://twitter.com/SmartMom8
Instagram
https://www.instagram.com/cwbnnetwork

Connect with the Contributing Authors Here

Kutana Counsil
https://www.facebook.com/kcdiva.lyfe
Bobbie Tomlin
https://www.facebook.com/bjtomlin84
Sharee Houston
https://www.facebook.com/sharee.houston.1
Jacqueline Goodwin
https://www.facebook.com/lenisegoodwin

Made in the
USA
Columbia, SC